true green life

true green life

in 100 everyday ways

Kim McKay and Jenny Bonnin

NATIONAL GEOGRAPHIC

WASHINGTON, D.C.

Published by the National Geographic Society

First Published in Australia by ABC Books in April 2009 for the Australian
Broadcasting Corporation.

Copyright © 2010 True Green (Global) Pty Ltd

ISBN 978-1-4262-0517-0

Cover Photo: Corbis Australia

Design and image selection by Marian Kyte
Research and editing by Helen Littleton

A percentage of the proceeds from the sale of *True Green Life*
benefits Clean Up the World.

True Green ® is a Trademark of True Green (Global) Pty Ltd.

The National Geographic Society is one of the world's largest nonprofit scientific
and educational organizations. Founded in 1888 to "increase and diffuse
geographic knowledge," the Society works to inspire people to care about the
planet. It reaches more than 325 million people worldwide each month through
its official journal, NATIONAL GEOGRAPHIC, and other magazines; National Geographic
Channel; television documentaries; music; radio; films; books; DVDs; maps;
exhibitions; school publishing programs; interactive media; and merchandise.
National Geographic has funded more than 9,000 scientific research, conservation
and exploration projects and supports an education program combating
geographic illiteracy. For more information, visit nationalgeographic.com.

For more information, please call 1-800-NGS LINE (647-5463)
or write to the following address:

National Geographic Society
1145 17th Street N.W.
Washington, D.C. 20036-4688 U.S.A.

Visit us online at www.nationalgeographic.com

Printed in China on recycled paper

09/PPS/1

The Internet, your local, state, and federal governments all produce
terrific information and advice on how to live a greener life, with
online journals, magazines, and websites dedicated to a greener
world. We gratefully acknowledge the valuable resources in the
research of *True Green Life* and encourage you to explore the
many sites listed on pages 124–134 for even more information
and inspiration to create a better and cleaner world.

contents

Wendy Gordon
Founder, *The Green Guide*

Recently I read that after more than a decade of blockbuster growth, U.S. bottled water sales dropped 6 percent this past year. Why? Because eco-minded consumers are rejecting bottled water as wasteful and turning to the tap. Way to go, people!

This is no trivial matter, you see. U.S. studies show that total energy required for bottled water production is as much as 2,000 times the energy needed in producing tap water. As for the water used by bottling industry: It takes three liters of water to produce one liter of water in the standard PET plastic, according to the Pacific Institute.

So, chalk one up for lots of individuals making one simple change in their everyday lives that's making a whole lot of difference for the planet.

What other ways can we make a difference? You'd be surprised. Virtually in every facet of daily life, there are countless ways to save energy, resources, and money as well. From the food you feed your family to the parties you throw on special occasions, you have choices, and making the smarter choices can make a lot of difference.

Here's the book to help you. *True Green Life in 100 Everyday Ways,* by my friends Kim McKay and Jenny Bonnin, makes it easy. To me, their latest addition to the True Green series is like a cookbook with a 100 recipes to green your daily life. None are too hard, or too costly. They just may require a slightly different set of ingredients or different ways of doing things than you're used to.

Here is an example: Rather than buy regular toilet tissues, switch to brands that are 100 percent recycled and unbleached. You'll be saving virgin old-growth forest.

Similarly, here's a good sense solution to skyrocketing energy bills: A few well-placed trees on the sunny side of the house can cut your air-conditioning needs by up to 75 percent.

The "recipes" in *True Green Life* will take you way beyond the home. Kim and Jenny also offer simple ways to green your travel or your next vacation. I love trains so I was particularly excited to read that they suggest taking the train when you next travel, whether for work or a vacation. The savings are tremendous and the views often exquisite. Trains can get you to the most amazing places, from seashores to national parks. And it's been my experience that trains are more comfortable, more fun, and more of an adventure.

Nor is any part of life beyond *True Green Life*'s scope. Take celebrations. From birthdays to weddings, it explores every aspect, from the plates and cups used at a birthday picnic in the park to the rings and dress selected for that most special of days—one's wedding.

There are few aspects of daily life where we couldn't be a bit greener. And few of the things we need to do to be greener require much effort. And most make such good sense that once we make these changes, they become second nature, and we forget what life was like before.

I applaud Kim and Jenny for their informed, common-sense approach to making green a part of daily life. *True Green Life* is simple, fun, engaging. And mark my words, whether it's filling your Thermos with tap water or stocking up on recycled toilet tissue, when each of us makes the smarter choice for ourselves, it means a world of good for everyone.

introduction

Kim McKay and Jenny Bonnin

Live the true green life!

Today it is so easy to be true green! We have the technology. We can choose from all kinds of renewable energy for our homes to save money and reduce carbon emissions. We have learned to walk more, to take public transportation, or to trade in our gas-guzzlers for more efficient cars. We just need to ensure that we actually do these things. That means we need to rethink how we live on the planet and realize how much more important it has become for us to care about the health of our world for future generations.

We live in challenging times, but most of all we live in a time when we have a chance to collectively make a critical difference in how others will live. We believe it is essential to live a true green life!

A true green life is also a smart life. It's about the informed choices we make. If more of us chose renewable energy to power our lifestyles—that's electricity from wind, solar, hydro, or geothermal power, or even from garbage—then it naturally follows that those industries would further prosper, energy from coal-fired power would be in less demand, and "green power" as we know it today would be affordable and would help create healthier communities.

The availability of green products is increasing every day. This makes it easier to live in an environmentally conscious way. Hybrid cars, which combine a gas engine with an electric motor, can save both dollars on fuel and greenhouse gas emissions. Non-toxic and eco-friendly cleaning products are widely available, and the

tipping point is not far off when "green homes" become the norm rather than the exception. Thankfully it has become a trend to use sustainable or recycled lumber, energy-efficient lighting, and eco-friendly, low-VOC (volatile organic compounds) paints for building and renovation projects.

If you want to try to live a true green life, it can be as simple as just changing a few habits. Conserve energy by not stressing about where to park in the city. Take public transportation, or walk; it feels good to exercise, and it saves money and reduces emissions, too. Really think about what you buy. When you decide it's annoying that you can't recycle Styrofoam meat trays, find an alternative: Shop at the local butcher. Analyzing the packaging you are offered is a great motivator for change. Think about it as a game, and whoever offers you less wins! Unplug every appliance or piece of equipment when you are not using it, whether it's a computer, cell-phone charger, or stereo—in fact, anything with a standby light, which uses energy and costs you money even when it is turned off. Water tanks make a lot of sense, too, if you have room to

< if you want to try to live a true green life, it can be as simple as just changing a few habits >

Photo: Corbis Australia

install one where you live. If that's not possible, then save water by taking shorter showers; even turning the faucet off when brushing your teeth will help conserve our most precious resource.

Creativity can also help with your habit-changing process. Consider the paper wasted from birthdays, holiday celebrations, and gifts for the new baby. Make wrapping "paper" from fabrics or other reusable materials. Dish towels can add usefulness and color to wedding gifts, place mats at dinner parties can be made from scraps of fabric or yarn, and cards can be made of recycled paper—or why not send an e-card? It's a challenge, but a fun one for the entire family. Can you go a whole month, or even a year, without buying wrapping paper?

And the last frontier is travel. We travel more than any generation before us. Put extra thought into your work or vacation travel. Preserving pristine wildernesses and appreciating conservation efforts through sustainable tourism operators is important in making sure our children and grandchildren are able to witness firsthand the wonders of our magnificent planet.

For a true green life, be aware of how we can all work with Mother Nature and not against her. Get in touch with your surroundings and learn from them. We wish you well in your endeavor to join our true green journey.

Today we travel more than any previous generation, so extra consideration about your carbon footprint is vital when planning a trip. Understand your natural environment, and support sustainable destinations whether you're traveling at home or overseas.

travel

1 practice responsible tourism

The average American has only two weeks of paid vacation a year, yet the amount of emissions produced by tourism is greater than the amount of emissions produced annually by billions of people living and working in big, industrialized countries and emerging economies. Since flying has the greatest environmental impact, try to combine trips and avoid stopovers (planes use a lot of fuel while taking off and landing). When you're planning your trip abroad, choose tourism operators and booking agents who have a strong environmental policy.

• *take vacations that give the world a break, too*

Photo: Corbis Australia

don't overpack

2

W hat you pack in your luggage has a direct impact on the environment. The more bags you take and the more you put into them, the more you are charged by the airline and the more jet fuel will be used. Be a light traveler. You don't have to take everything. To avoid taking unnecessary items, research your destination before you go and know what the weather will be like. Not all countries or destinations have sophisticated waste management or recycling facilities. Avoid disposable items, substitute biodegradable products (especially eco-friendly soap) in your toiletries bag, and take clothes that don't require heavy laundering.

• *avoid excess baggage, which can cost you and the environment*

Photo: Corbis Australia

before you leave

3

Whether you are away for a weekend or for a month, remember to put your house into "energy hibernation." Switch off all lights, and turn off and unplug electrical appliances. You will save energy, your house will be safer, and your utility bill will be lower. For extended trips, it's worth turning off your electric hot water heater, too. Longer vacations can be a great opportunity to empty and defrost your fridge and freezer—particularly if you have a manual-defrost model. Frost buildup increases the amount of energy the motor must use to keep running. And don't forget to suspend your subscription to the morning newspaper while you're away!

• *shut down your home while you're away*

Illustration: Marian Kyte

4

a paperless vacation?

Forget collecting a bundle of brochures from your travel agent. Instead, use the vast resources of the Internet, your local public library, and well-traveled friends (and bloggers) to plan and book your next vacation. Everything from researching your destination to booking travel, accommodations, and tours can be done online. Save time, paper, resources, and associated CO_2 emissions. Most airlines, travel agents, and tourist bureau websites give you the option of e-brochures, e-zines, and subscriptions to e-newsletters with all the information and deals you need. Convert to e-ticketing, and use online check-in counters; it will save you time in line, too!

• *actively reduce vacation paperwork*

Illustration: Marian Kyte

5
be an ecotourist

See the world in a different way. Make sure your vacations are about appreciation and conservation, not commercialization and exploitation. The International Ecotourism Society (TIES) promotes ecotourism by educating tourists and tourism professionals in responsible, culturally aware, and sustainable travel and in helping to conserve the environment and the welfare of local communities. Choose tour operators, accommodations, and attractions that are members of TIES, are certified by the Sustainable Tourism Eco-Certification Program (STEP), or follow the Global Sustainable Tourism Criteria (GSTC), so that your travels can have a positive impact on local communities and the environment.

* *support ecotourism in your accommodations and tour choices*

Photo: Corbis Australia

eco-accommodations

6

We all love going on vacation, but one of the challenges is to make sure we don't damage the habitats of endangered plants and animals while we are on the road. We know the impact humans have on the health of our planet, and fortunately there are ways to enjoy vacations without harming the environment. There are now specially designed vacation resorts, farm stays, and tours that have demonstrated green credentials and are guaranteed to be ecologically sustainable. Check out your favorite vacation destination and see if it is "eco-aware." If not, look for ecotours available in that area.

• *book an eco-friendly vacation*

travel and tourism calculations

7

Don't just check the exchange rate when you're deciding where to go on your next vacation. Calculate and compare your potential tourism carbon footprint. You can find many helpful travel and tourism calculators on the Internet to determine the greenhouse gas emissions associated with your proposed travel options. A calculator will help you compare the potential CO_2 emissions from your vacation plans, including accommodations (hostels versus five-star hotels), transportation (flying versus driving or boating), and recreation (visiting theme parks versus hiking or cycling tours). Then you can make the most positive choices in terms of how you get around, where you stay, and what you do.

• *plan to take the greenest route possible*

8

a new way to fly

Sometimes there's no alternative to flying, but with a long-haul flight producing more than four tons of CO_2 (and over one ton of carbon), you should always fly "carbon neutral" by offsetting your flight emissions. Most major airlines now provide carbon-offset opportunities to make your flight greener. A small contribution, incorporated into the cost of your ticket, can compensate for the portion of your flight-related carbon emissions. These offsets, via the airline's green partnerships, contribute to tree-planting programs and other renewable energy projects. Check to see if your preferred carrier offers an offset program, and include the cost of offsetting your flight in your travel budget.

• plant a tree and invest in renewable energy whenever you fly

9

support public transportation

Public transportation isn't only for getting you to work. It's just as important while you're traveling. Not only can it add to your adventure, it's greener and cheaper than renting a car or catching a taxi. Make sure to ask your travel agent about public transportation options at your destination before you go. Also, use public transportation for your airport transfers as an easy, green option. Many major airports located near metropolitan areas have good public transportation to get you to your downtown hotel.

- *vacation with public transportation*

Photo: Corbis Australia

10

grand journeys

Taking a train can be romantic, and it is one of the most eco-friendly ways to travel. Catching the train from San Francisco to Los Angeles saves twice the carbon dioxide used to fly. Take some of the world's greatest train trips; in doing so, you'll see more of the world, you'll be kinder to the environment, and you'll support local economies and communities. Crisscross Europe with Eurostar and the *Venice Simplon-Orient-Express*. The *Rocky Mountaineer* and the *Canadian* can show you Canada and the Rockies up close. The *Ghan* and the *Indian Pacific* take you into the Australian outback. Amtrak, the Durango & Silverton Railroad, and the California *Zephyr* will show you the heart of the United States. And you can get to Washington, D.C., from Boston for that sightseeing trip faster than driving and in a more eco-friendly fashion by taking the Acela. It's more relaxing, more fun, and the greener way to go!

11

avoid expansive trips

We travel more than any previous generation has, and the collective impact of transporting people to their vacation destinations—and accommodating them—means global tourism is becoming one of the world's biggest polluters. You don't have to go overseas to take a break. Choose low-carbon vacations closer to home, such as camping and cycling trips, which can have close to zero emissions, and, when you can, take the train or bus instead of getting on a plane. If you're planning a short break or getaway, think simple and local for a cleaner, more relaxing vacation.

• *reduce your vacation's total emissions beyond just your flights*

Photo: Corbis Australia

12

be a low-carbon tourist

Being on vacation isn't an excuse to take a break from being true green! Whether you are a guest or a host, don't forget to be green and energy efficient. Help your guests lighten their luggage by supplying fresh towels and even some eco-friendly toiletries. When you're abroad, help your hotel managers and innkeepers become greener. Do you really need to have your sheets and towels changed every day? Unplug appliances you're not using, and switch off lights in your hotel room while you're out exploring. Take your own toiletries, take short showers, and pack rechargeable batteries for your digital camera equipment.

- *reduce your impact at home and abroad*

13 slow travel

In our rush to get to our vacation destinations, we forget how much fun the actual journey can be. You can see a lot of the world without flying, and your vacation experience can be a lot more memorable and adventurous. Go overland, or take the scenic route to a destination, and immerse yourself in the local culture along the way. You'll see little towns, undiscovered gems, and amazing people you would normally just fly over. You'd be surprised how easy it can be to travel all over the world without flying: Take a yacht or catch a ferry to see the Greek islands, hop a train to explore the United States or Europe, or jump on local buses to see South America and Asia.

• *really see the world by choosing not to fly*

Photo: Corbis Australia

be a good traveler

Responsible tourism is about being culturally sensitive as much as it is about being ecologically aware. Before you venture overseas, or even to remote parts of North America, read about where you are going, its history, its local culture, and its politics. Always respect the customs of the area you're visiting, and dress appropriately, particularly when visiting religious or cultural sites. Brush up on the local language, and always learn the basics; being able to greet people and say "please" and "thank you" in the local language shows you are polite and respectful of their culture. And don't forget that a smile works in any language.

• *respect different cultures and customs*

Illustration: Marian Kyte

MY GREEN PASSPORT

thank you
cheers
do je
danke
gracias
tak
Xie Xie

don't be a souvenir hunter

Your tourism dollars make an important contribution to a local community's economy, but spend them wisely so they benefit the local community. In situations where it is customary to haggle, always pay a fair price—don't over-haggle or you could be unfairly taking advantage of the seller's situation. Choose souvenirs that don't exploit or deplete local wildlife or flora. International wildlife legislation and customs restrictions may not allow you to import items such as ivory, tortoiseshell, and coral when you return home. Always make positive souvenir choices that support local craftspeople instead of purchasing plastic or "touristy" items that are more than likely imported.

• *choose your souvenirs sensitively and buy ethically*

Photo: Marian Kyte

16
be a supportive tourist

Do as the locals do, and help generate income and employment for local communities. Make an effort to discover the flavor and authentic culture and lifestyle of your vacation destination. Enjoy and learn about foods from local markets, street vendors, and restaurants rather than always eating at your hotel. If you're on an all-inclusive vacation package, make sure you venture outside the resort so you can take advantage of opportunities offered by local people. By directly engaging with the locals, your tourism dollar will have a direct and positive impact on people's lives. Of course, you should always check with your hotel staff regarding city areas and neighborhoods that may not be safe for exploring.

- *get out and connect with local cultures*

17

culture club

If you're visiting sites of national significance, use a reputable tour operator or guide with the appropriate accreditation to ensure that your visit has no negative impact. Most countries have very strict laws to protect their cultural property. You may unknowingly purchase artifacts or antiques of historical or cultural importance (and this may, in turn, encourage theft). Don't rely on the assurances of street traders and shopkeepers. Check before you buy. Strict exportation and importation laws may apply—and even if they don't, consider the ethics of removing objects of cultural significance from communities or countries in order to decorate your house or garden.

• *respect the history of your travel destinations*

Photo: Corbis Australia

declare it

Be aware of immigration rules before bringing items back from abroad. When you get home, you must declare all agricultural items, including fruits, vegetables, plants, soil, meats, and any other animal products. These items, along with gifts or souvenirs purchased overseas—especially those made from animal by-products—can't be brought into the United States because they may carry highly contagious pests and diseases that, once introduced into the country, could have devastating effects on the agricultural and tourism industries and indigenous flora and fauna. Many of these items may also be prohibited under wildlife legislation or require import permits. To be certain, check regulations before you go.

• *respect and comply with customs and quarantine regulations*

19

under the sea

Discovering the world's coral reefs and oceans can be one of the best vacation activities you'll ever experience. But when you plan your next diving or snorkeling trip, also arrange to volunteer a bit of your time while you are there. As a recreational scuba diver or snorkeler, you can take part in significant local and global research projects. Volunteer for a reef cleanup and record observational data for marine conservation; you will help preserve the health and diversity of our oceans and reefs. Always respect local guidelines and regulations. Wear waterproof sunscreen to protect your skin. Explore gently, avoid stepping on the reefs, don't touch (or remove) the coral, and don't feed the fish.

• ***monitor and conserve marine life on your dive trip***

Photos: (top) Surfers Paradise, Tourism Queensland; (below) Great Barrier Reef, Tourism Queensland

leave only your footprint

20

You don't want your own environment covered in trash, so be careful not to leave anything behind when you visit the world's natural wonders. If you're camping, think about how you can use water for washing dishes and keeping clean without damaging the environment. Then there's the question of using the toilet. If there are no bathrooms provided, make sure you use a spot at least 100 yards from the campsite and away from rivers and creeks—and bury everything at least six inches deep. Don't disturb the local plants or animals, and don't feed the wildlife. Stick to well-defined paths and beach access points, and don't deface or disrupt anything. Leave it all just as you found it.

• *respect the world and leave places as you found them*

Photo: Boulia, Tourism Queensland

Celebrate life and mark special occasions, but also consider how your event will impact the environment. Rethink your consumption of party supplies, such as disposable paper plates and plastic knives, forks, and spoons. Look for better alternatives to reduce waste without reducing the fun.

celebrations

life

memories

birth *hope*

loss *love*

a family tree tradition

Throughout our lives, there is a lot to celebrate and a lot to mourn. Start a green tradition in your family to mark major events. To celebrate, to remember, and to remind—there are a lot of good reasons to plant a tree. Mark the births of your children or the loss of a loved one, your child's first and last day of school, college graduations, weddings, and even divorces. You'll be creating tangible touchstones for you and your family and helping to protect the environment.

• *mark important events by planting a tree for a cleaner future*

true green party

M ore than 15 trees are cut down to make every ton of the coated, higher-end virgin paper used for magazines, catalogs, and greeting cards. In 2008 more than 57 percent of the paper consumed in the United States was recovered for recycling—a record amount—but we still have a long way to go. The next time you organize a birthday party, housewarming party, or barbecue, make it green. Think about what makes a great party and how much stuff gets thrown away afterward. Use recycled materials for costumes, decorations, and wrapping paper. Provide locally grown organic food, and don't serve it on disposable plates. Let people know that it's a green party when you invite them, and encourage them to follow your lead.

• *have a party for the environment*

Photo: Corbis Australia

23

the bride wore green

Your big day is big business: The average American wedding now costs a whopping $28,000. Make sure you plan your wedding so it doesn't cost the world—literally. If you use a wedding planner or a gift registry, make green choices. For the all-important dress, go vintage; recycle or alter an existing dress. Or, for something new, choose earth-friendly fabrics. Catering can easily be organic. Your wedding stationery can be 100 percent recycled. And wedding favors can be environmentally thoughtful. For the deeply committed, try for a carbon-neutral wedding and reduce the travel distance for guests, or ask them to purchase carbon offsets for their travel in lieu of buying you a wedding present!

• *vow to have an eco-wedding*

i will and i do

Diamonds are important to Africa's prosperity. But the illegal trade of rough diamonds has fueled decades of devastating conflict in countries such as Angola and Sierra Leone. Ensure that your diamond's journey from the mine to your finger is conflict free. The Kimberley Process Certification Scheme (KPCS) is an international initiative, backed by the United Nations, to stem the trade in conflict diamonds. If you are in the market for a diamond, only buy from suppliers who can guarantee that their diamonds are conflict free. Think green for your wedding bands, too. Gold mining is one of the world's dirtiest industries. The production of a single wedding band can generate 22 tons of mine waste. It might be greener to choose a kinder alternative such as an antique or an heirloom ring.

• invest in a conflict-free diamond—commit to each other and a better world

functional flowers

When you're ordering flowers for a special event such as a wedding, choose a florist who supports organic, seasonal, and local flowers; that way you can be sure to reduce the associated environmental costs of long-distance transportation. Select flowers that are in season—a bridal bouquet of hydrangeas or peonies would be glorious for a summer wedding, and boutonnieres made of local blooms will look great on groomsmen. For table settings at wedding receptions or other functions, choose imaginative live options, such as forced bulbs like hyacinths or miniature pots of herbs that guests can take with them. At the end of the day, why not donate the flower arrangements to the local church or a local hospital to spread the joy that flowers bring?

• *flowers shouldn't fly—keep them local*

Photo: Marian Kyte

green honeymooners

26

Considering the environment is now a big factor in many couples' wedding plans—and that includes the honeymoon. In fact, there's a booming industry for very romantic, and very green, honeymoon getaways closer to home. Even if you want some unabashed luxury, many major domestic hotel chains have introduced green business practices. Check out their credentials. And if you want to avoid mass tourism after the big day, you'll have plenty of choices, with more secluded, eco-friendly special occasion destinations opening all the time. If you're going to fly, make sure you include carbon offsets when booking your tickets.

• *stay true green when choosing the hotel suite or a wilderness retreat*

27
welcome baby

Introduce your baby to the world—and green ethics—with an eco-shower. And make the important milestones in your baby's life—his or her birth, christening or baptism, bris, or other naming ceremony—more about the collective goodwill of friends and family and less about gifts and consumerism. Throw an eco-shower with fun green themes like "organic only," "pre-loved clothing and accessories," or "frozen meals for sleep-deprived parents." Encourage guests to think eco-friendly, too, by wrapping any presents in cloth diapers or burp cloths to avoid extra waste.

• *start your baby with the right footprint*

Photo: Marian Kyte

happy birthday

28

Disposable cups, plates, hats, napkins, and party decorations are the essentials of a low-hassle child's birthday party. But unless you make greener choices, many of these items will still be in landfills when your child celebrates his or her 90th birthday. Avoid disposable plastic, polystyrene, and non-recycled paper products altogether; they're not biodegradable. For party basics, look for bio-plastics and natural fiber ware made from corn, sugar cane, and bamboo, or 100 percent recycled paper products that are tree-friendly, biodegradable, or recyclable. Buy birthday candles made of soy or beeswax. Traditional candles are often made from paraffin, which is derived from petroleum. Then make a birthday wish for a greener and cleaner future.

• *find green solutions to your party needs*

29

eco-friendly invites and cards

All your stationery needs, such as cards, invitations, and thank-you notes, can be made from recycled paper or made by you. For your next party, make invitations with recycled materials. Look for eco-friendly, "tree-free," or 100 percent recycled paper options. Or why not go paper free and send e-cards and e-invites from your blog or Facebook page? If you still need paper cards for low-tech relatives, make sure they are recycled, or send charity-based cards.

• *send a message to save paper*

Illustration: Marian Kyte

gifts that keep giving

30

What do you buy for a person who has everything? How about a mosquito net for a family in Uganda? A goat for a mother in Bangladesh? Or even a beehive for a community in Tanzania? Oxfam America, Heifer International, World Vision, and the United Nations Children's Fund (UNICEF) all have catalogs of life-changing gifts to help relieve poverty and the pressures on our environment. Give twice—to your loved one and to someone with not much at all. In Africa, where a child dies of malaria every 30 seconds, that mosquito net will keep a family safer from infection. These unique gifts will help to improve the health and well-being of a community, family, or individual, and they will improve sustainability in countries all over the world.

• *give a gift twice—give a goat*

Illustration: Marian Kyte

31

the joy of giving

There is something special—and green—about gifts you've made yourself, and they're extra special if they're made from recycled materials. The gift of your time and talent is more meaningful than another store-bought CD. The number of gifts you can make is only limited by your imagination: Cook up a storm and make a batch of cookies or delectable jams and preserves, or create your own potted plants from seeds or cuttings. You can also give gifts in kind. How about a night of free babysitting for a friend with young children, or mowing the lawn for your elderly neighbor's birthday? Give a gift with a personal, earth-friendly touch.

• *give the gift worth giving*

32

my green valentine

Valentine's Day is a special day on everyone's calendar. It can also be your chance to say "I love you" to the environment and to say no to poverty. More than 40 percent of the world's chocolate that is not organic or Fair Trade comes from the Ivory Coast, which has a history of unfair and exploitative labor practices. On one of the biggest shopping days of the year, make sure your consumer dollars are going where they can do the most good; buy organic and Fair Trade–certified chocolates, so you know the farmer has received a fair price for his crop. And buy organic, local flowers for your sweetie to reduce toxic pesticides and associated transportation emissions.

- *give "green" chocolates to your sweetheart*

mother's day

Officially celebrated in the United States since 1914, Mother's Day grew out of a pacifist movement following the carnage of the Civil War. The founders of modern Mother's Day, Julia Ward Howe and Anna Jarvis, never could have imagined how their day would become a billion-dollar industry, one of consumerism and waste. Honor your mother this Mother's Day in the tradition of the day's founders: Make it a special day about peace and family. Let your mother know how important she is in your life; you don't have to buy something to do that. You could cook her breakfast or dinner, spend the day with her, help her around the house, or make a Mother's Day resolution to be there more for her in the year ahead.

• *tell your mother she's special—without the waste*

Photo: Marian Kyte

you're the best 34
father's day

Something as small as a disposable razor can be a big problem for the environment. About two billion disposable razors end up in U.S. landfills every year. Like so many things labeled as disposable, they simply aren't; the little plastic parts and handles don't break down when you throw them away. Opt for a cleaner shave by making a more sustainable choice of razor. A rechargeable electric shaver can last for years, and you won't need shaving cream. If you do go disposable, choose a razor that allows you to change the blades or has recyclable parts.

• *help Dad get a truly clean—and green—shave*

35
eco-thanksgiving dinner

These holidays, plan to celebrate local food, in the true tradition of a harvest festival, by having a sustainable Thanksgiving dinner. Since the 1960s, the broad-breasted, white industrial breed of turkey has dominated our supermarkets—a far cry from the turkey our great-grandparents would have enjoyed. Make sure the centerpiece of your Thanksgiving dinner is an authentic heritage turkey that is organic, free-range, and free of chemicals and hormones—not from a factory. But put your order in early; the heritage turkey has a slower growth rate than its commercial counterpart. Find your heritage turkey from a certified producer to enjoy its full flavor and to support a humane, environmentally sensitive poultry farmer. And don't forget to buy your Thanksgiving vegetables and all the trimmings from local markets.

• *make your star attraction a genuine heritage turkey*

Photo: Corbis Australia

Illustration: Marian Kyte

36

festive glow

Decorating houses with lights has become a big part of the American holiday season. Make sure you power up your home's holiday display with responsible energy by switching to green power. Switch to energy-saving, LED mini-lights to decorate your tree and house. They look just as good, use less than 10 percent of the power of incandescent lights, and last 100 times longer. They're also safer and stay cooler—they won't singe the tree or your child's fingers. Don't forget to include a timer to shut off your lights automatically overnight or in the hours when no one's admiring your tree or yard display.

• *switch to energy-efficient holiday lights*

o christmas tree

In 2007, some 31.3 million trees were felled so that Americans could celebrate Christmas. That's a lot of Christmas trees. But which is greener, a real or artificial Christmas tree? The argument is not quite as straightforward as you may think. In obtaining your real tree, consider the gasoline used while shopping each year, the fuel used to transport the tree, and the energy used in its disposal. Then compare that to the petroleum used to make an artificial tree, the fuel used to ship it, and the fuel you use to shop for it. Remember, an artificial tree lasts for up to 15 years. Then there are also the petrochemicals used to manufacture fake trees—but also pesticides and fertilizers to grow the real ones. The whole debate is something of a conundrum. Make your tree choices wisely, taking into account the origin of your tree, the products used in its growth and manufacture, and its subsequent disposal. Or you could forgo tradition altogether—decorate a potted palm or a rosemary shrub. You can then plant the rosemary in your backyard to soak up carbon dioxide and to use in your holiday cooking for many more Christmases to come.

• *make your Christmas tree selection an informed one*

Photo: Corbis Australia

38
recycling holiday cheer

After the holidays have passed, annual season's greetings cards can keep spreading good wishes. Programs such as the St. Jude's Ranch Recycling Card Program give people from all over the world a way to keep giving. Millions of Americans have donated their previous year's Christmas cards so that they could be turned into "new" cards for the coming season by the children at St. Jude's. Countless greeting cards and envelopes have been recycled, saving millions of trees in the process. It is easy to recycle your cards. Any used, all-occasion greeting cards may be sent to the St. Jude's Ranch for Children or recycled via your curbside recycling program.

- *have a green holiday, and help save millions of trees*

Each year, Americans use about 18 billion disposable diapers annually and throw 1.5 to 1.8 million tons of computers and other electronics into landfills. Every member of the family contributes to the household footprint. We all must do our part to reduce our families' impact.

family

grandma was right

39

It seems our grandparents were the original greenies. The lessons we were taught as children, such as "waste not, want not," have turned out to be environmental wisdom. In our modern lives we've become dependent upon a convenience culture, with an excess of plastics and chemicals—and it's costing our planet. Take the lead from our grandparents and previous generations, and reinstate resourcefulness. Our lives will be simpler, and maybe even a little richer, for it. You don't need to *buy* solutions to all your problems; you can make, mend, sew, cook, bake, and repair things yourself.

- *improvise to make something from nothing*

Photo: Marian Kyte

it's (not) a wrap

40

M any of our everyday kitchen items are non-recyclable and contain harmful chemicals. Make sure your food-storage bags and containers are made from safer plastics, like products made from polyethylene. Avoid containers made of number 3 plastics (like PVC vinyl), number 6 plastics (including polystyrene), or number 7 plastics (such as polycarbonate). Glass containers with removable lids are greener and just as convenient for storing food. Cover bowls with a plate rather than using aluminum foil or plastic wrap, and avoid commercial-grade cling wrap; it's usually made of vinyl. Look for 100 percent recycled aluminum foil and parchment paper made from unbleached paper. Wash and reuse wraps, foils, and food-storage bags instead of throwing them out after a single use.

• *find better alternatives to store your food*

Photo: Marian Kyte

41

the great outdoors

The energy used each year for cooking in the average American kitchen represents 4.5 percent of the home's total energy use, which means that among your stovetop, microwave, and oven, a lot of greenhouse gases are being produced. Take advantage of your outdoor grill for everyday meals. Cooking outside allows you to keep kitchen lights and exhaust fans off. You'll have fewer lingering odors in your home, and cleaning up will be easier, too. Reduce cooking time by thawing food first, and cook smaller amounts of food with a toaster oven, which requires less energy than a traditional oven. And remember, cleaner appliances mean more efficient energy use.

- *substitute the grill for the stove*

Photo: Corbis Australia

green your chores

More than 300 man-made chemicals can be found in our bodies—chemicals that people weren't exposed to just three generations ago. Play it safe and find natural alternatives; you don't need all those powerful chemicals to clean your house. Baking soda and vinegar is just as effective for household tasks. Substitute natural germ fighters such as lemon juice or hydrogen peroxide for bleach and chlorine—they're healthier and don't contribute to indoor pollution. Do a little bit every day, and regularly wipe down surfaces so grime doesn't build up. Also, make sure the detergents you use are biodegradable and have a low phosphorus content.

• *use eco-friendly cleaning methods*

Illustration: Marian Kyte

flushed away

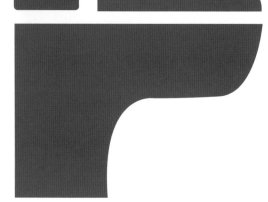

Toilet flushing is responsible for about one-third of all water used by the average U.S. household. Americans could save almost two billion gallons of water per day by replacing older toilets with newer, high-efficiency toilets. The dual-flush toilet, a technology new to the United States but used widely in Australia and Europe for years, uses between 4 quarts and 1 gallon per flush compared to 3.5 to 7 gallons in an older, single-flush toilet. If you're stuck with your old toilet, place an inexpensive toilet dam (available from hardware stores) in the tank to reduce the amount of water in each flush, or fill an empty soft-drink bottle and place that in the tank. Check for leaks, since they can waste up to 500 gallons of water a day! And don't forget to use recycled, unbleached, chlorine-free toilet paper. Some 424,000 trees could be saved every year if every U.S. household replaced just one 500-sheet roll of virgin-fiber toilet paper with a 100 percent recycled roll. But less than two percent of toilet paper used in the United States is 100 percent recycled; the vast majority is made from virgin and natural forests.

• *install a dual-flush toilet—save 264 gallons of water a year*

Photo: Shutterstock

44

ease the load

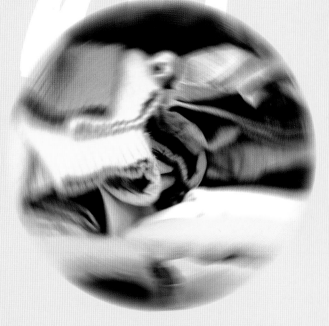

The average washing machine produces nearly 200 pounds of greenhouse gases a year. If you add hot water production, that's another 275 pounds of emissions. Be sure to choose the cold cycle, and you'll reduce the energy needed to wash your clothes by as much as 90 percent. If you're upgrading, buy a front-loading washing machine, which can use 50 percent less energy and 40 to 75 percent less water (about 26,500 fewer gallons) than a top-loading machine. Front loaders also use less detergent, and every 3.5 ounces of detergent can generate nearly 3 pounds of greenhouse gases in the manufacturing process. Only use what you need, choose detergent that is biodegradable with a low phosphorus content, and only wash full loads of clothing.

• *wash in cold water—save energy and money*

45 natural baby

As a proud parent, you and your bundle of joy are a marketer's dream. New products are devised for your every whim. But don't fall prey to such marketing ploys; aim to reduce the waste associated with your baby's needs and reduce exposure to harmful chemicals and toxins. Always look for baby toys made without PVC or other plastics. When you can, rent toys and equipment. When traveling, rent car-safety seats from your rental car agency or specialty rental companies. Reduce your need for infant formula and bottles. Breast milk is the ultimate renewable resource.

• *don't buy into the billion-dollar baby industry*

Photo: Corbis Australia

eco-friendly family pet

46

Don't forget the fluffy, four-legged members of your family. Go green for everything from toys and treats to collars and leashes to pet beds. Spoil your pets with a little home cooking and avoid large quantities of commercial pet food—it can contain questionable by-products. Research suitable pet food recipes online, or ask your vet for suggestions. Human food scraps can be a healthy alternative. For pet care and grooming needs, look for low-toxic and herbal flea and tick remedies and shampoos. When it comes to choosing kitty litter, avoid non-biodegradable products; make a biodegradable and organic choice.

• *green your pet's diet and health care*

47
lighten your lead foot

The way you drive can make a big difference in the amount of fuel you use. By accelerating slowly, driving at moderate speed, and avoiding the need for hard braking, you can dramatically increase the miles you get from a tank of fuel. Avoid high speeds: Every 5 mph you drive over 60 mph can decrease the miles per gallon your car will get by 7 to 8 percent. In addition, a cold engine is far less fuel efficient than a warmed-up engine; one multi-use car ride will consume only half the fuel of several short trips covering the same overall distance. Plan your journey to combine multiple errands, and avoid peak-hour traffic. Keeping your car well maintained, and making sure tires are inflated to the correct level, also helps fuel efficiency.

- *drive responsibly to lower vehicle emissions*

Photo: Corbis Australia

fuel for thought

48

If you can't afford a hybrid, you can still have an eco-efficient car. In 2003, the transportation sector was responsible for 27 percent of total greenhouse gas emissions in the United States. But a new Environmental Protection Agency (EPA) initiative aims to reduce this contribution. As of September 2008, all new cars sold are required to display a Fuel Economy Label, so you can easily compare the fuel efficiency levels across vehicles. This label, along with the EPA's Green Vehicle Guide website, rates all new cars by efficiency, air pollution, and greenhouse gas performance. On the website you can also check the fuel consumption of older vehicles, from the year 2000 on.

• find a car that's good for your needs and the environment

MADE IN

PRESERVATIVES
COLORINGS
ADDITIVES

CONTAINS
TRACES OF

49

always read
the label

A simple label can tell you a lot. By knowing a product's origin and contents, you can make informed choices to minimize potential health, environmental, and ethical risks. Take into account impacts associated with the manufacture, use, and disposal of the products you use. Knowing the actual ingredients in a product is important in avoiding food additives that can be associated with allergies such as asthma or eczema. Knowing where your jeans or sneakers are made can make the difference between supporting unfair work practices and promoting responsible industry. If you really know what is in your cosmetic, cleaning, and home maintenance products, you might think—and purchase— differently. Look for greener alternatives and be a conscious consumer: Understand what it is you're really buying.

• *know the green credentials of products you use*

Illustration: Marian Kyte

50
green at peace

Environmentally considerate funerals and burials are gaining in popularity. A single cremation produces about 353 pounds of carbon dioxide. Traditional burials also produce roughly 86 pounds of greenhouse gases due to the maintenance of cemetery grounds and the building of headstones. Ask a funeral director about available green options. Traditional coffins and caskets, made from hardwoods and metals, can be substituted with 100 percent recycled corrugated cardboard coffins. They're non-toxic, biodegradable, and compliant with the legal and occupational health and safety standards of the U.S. funeral industry. Include your favorite charity in your will, and consider requesting that mourners make donations to charity rather than purchasing flowers.

- *reduce the final footprint of a loved one with an eco-funeral*

More than 270 million pounds of medications end up in our waterways and landfills every year, and nearly 8 out of every 10 bottles—of the approximately 28 billion plastic water bottles Americans buy every year—end up in a landfill. Correct disposal and vigilant recycling are important lessons for a healthier life. Pass it on!

health

the famous five

Most of us only eat half the amount of fruits and vegetables recommended for a balanced, healthy diet. In the United States, a staggering 66 percent of adults—two out of every three—are overweight or obese, and nearly one in five children is overweight. The growing rate of obesity is a serious health issue and creates a big drain on the planet's resources. Include a variety of foods from each of the five food groups (grains, fruits, vegetables, meat and beans, and dairy) into your diet every day. These foods provide the nutrients our bodies need for optimum health. Limit snacks and treats, and don't forget to drink lots of water. And exercise!

• *choose fruits and veggies over processed snacks and fast foods*

Photo: Corbis Australia

go organic

W e are what we eat. There is no comparison between commercial agriculture—a big user of fossil fuels, synthetic pesticides, hormones, and antibiotics—and organic agriculture, which uses natural pesticides, supports healthy soils, and works in harmony with the seasons. You could grow a vegetable patch in your backyard or plant some fruit trees to create your own organic produce. Organic food not only tastes better, but also contains more beneficial nutrients and minerals. On your next trip to the grocery store, look for organic alternatives, and remember that all truly organic foods and products are certified by the U.S. Department of Agriculture (USDA) National Organic Program, so look for the "USDA Organic" label.

• *eat, shop, and live organic*

Photo: Corbis Australia

53

mother's milk

Breast milk has a wide range of benefits for your baby's health, nutrition, and development. When possible and practical, choose breast over bottle for at least the first six months of your baby's life. If you are bottle-feeding, choose bottles, nipples, and containers made of tempered glass or safer plastics such as polyethylene or polypropylene (recycling symbol 1, 2, or 5). Avoid polycarbonate baby bottles (containing bisphenol A, or BPA) and bottles made from polyvinyl chloride (PVC), as some of these items may contain toxic chemicals that can leach into infant formula when sterilized and heated. With the boom in organics, it is now easy to choose organic infant formula, food, and snacks for your baby.

• *make the natural and renewable choice*

Photo: Corbis Australia

bless you and
gesundheit!

54

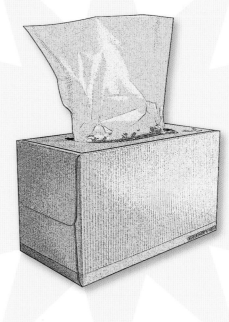

The environmental impact of disposable facial tissues is nothing to sneeze at. Support tissue manufacturers with high recycled content and clean manufacturing processes. Make sure your next box is unbleached and 100 percent recycled—otherwise you'll be contributing to the destruction of virgin or old-growth forests. Look for products labeled "totally chlorine-free (TCF)" or "processed chlorine-free (PCF)." Forgo those days when you're tucked in bed with a runny nose and a box of tissues. Revive the handkerchief, and take some sensible hygienic precautions. Try using hankies only once and laundering them instead of reusing them. And consider blowing your nose with recycled toilet paper to save even more packaging—it's ultimately all the same paper, anyway.

• *use 100 percent recycled tissues*

Illustration: Marian Kyte

55

see into the future

In North America alone, over four million pairs of eyeglasses are simply thrown away each year. Yet millions of people around the world, particularly in Africa, Asia, and Latin America, don't have access to basic eye care, let alone glasses. The World Health Organization (WHO) estimates that 153 million people have uncorrected refractive errors (nearsightedness, farsightedness, and astigmatism), all of which are easily remedied with glasses. Your unwanted glasses and nonprescription sunglasses can be recycled and reused. Donate them to one of the many charities that manage dedicated recycling programs, such as Lions Recycle for Sight and Unite for Sight. Access to glasses for anyone, young or old, can mean independence and greater opportunities.

• *donate unwanted glasses—improve someone else's life*

Photo: Corbis Australia

common sense for colds

Cold medications are a multi-million-dollar industry. A lot of energy goes into the production, packaging, and distribution of medicines that don't cure the cold, so perhaps a strong dose of prevention is a greener way to deal with the two to four colds we catch per year. As a first step, practice good hygiene to avoid catching and spreading germs. Wash your hands frequently with soap; keep them away from your eyes, nose, and mouth; and don't share cups, dishes, and utensils. If you do catch a cold, get some rest, drink plenty of fluids, and let your immune system fight the cold. Be sure to always consult with your physician or pharmacist if your symptoms come on suddenly, are severe, or last longer than usual.

- *avoid pharmaceuticals to treat common colds*

mercury-free health care

57

Mercury (Hg) can be found in many consumer and health products in your home, at your physician's office, and even in the fish you eat. Many common household and health care products contain mercury—items such as thermometers, blood pressure devices, batteries, electrical switches, fluorescent lights (including CFLs), and even some toys and jewelry. Significant exposure to mercury has serious health and ecological effects. The amount of mercury in just one fever thermometer, disposed of improperly, is enough to contaminate fish in a 20-acre lake. Reduce your use of products containing mercury, and properly dispose of them. Find safer alternatives such as a digital thermometer, know how to properly clean up a broken mercury thermometer spill (never use a vacuum cleaner), and choose low-mercury fish for meals, particularly if you are pregnant or have small children.

• *eliminate mercury from health care waste*

Photo: Corbis Australia

avoid the headache

Careless disposal of unwanted and expired medicines is an environmental and health hazard—and it's a huge problem in the United States. Medicines contain highly soluble chemicals that can pollute waterways, harm aquatic life, and even end up in our drinking water if they're flushed down the toilet, poured in the sink, or tossed in the garbage. Currently, there are no national guidelines for disposal of old medications. Try contacting your pharmacy to see if they have a drug-recycling program (many do). Your local hazardous waste facility may have a disposal site. If all else fails, mix the medicines with an inedible substance like coffee grounds or kitty litter, seal them in their original container, place the container in a sealed bag, and discard it in the trash.

• *reduce the more than 270 million pounds of medications in our waterways and landfills*

get personal

59

We all use soap and other personal-care products to keep ourselves clean and healthy. However, many toiletries and cosmetics contain chemicals that have not been tested adequately and could cause health problems, not only for people but also for the planet. Everything you put on your skin ends up in your body, so always choose natural and organic over synthetic products. Also keep in mind that products labeled "natural" are not certified the way organic products are—many contain just one or two natural ingredients. Be an attentive consumer; always check for certification.

• *choose organic skin-care products*

Photo: Corbis Australia

a radical hairstyle

60

Americans wash their hair nearly five times a week, but our scalps are under attack from the overuse of shampoos, which can conspire to alter our skin's natural oils. Shampoo is, after all, a detergent. The scalp can dry out, fostering skin conditions such as eczema, psoriasis, and dandruff. One answer, and a plus for the environment and your wallet, is to stop using shampoo. Join the "no 'poo" movement; let your hair find its natural balance by using milder substances (such as baking soda, lemon juice, or vinegar) to clean your locks. A number of people have tried no-shampoo living and love the way their hair looks and feels—and they are not putting toxins on their heads or washing them down the shower drain.

• *join the no-shampoo revolution*

hidden beauty

Our consumer culture is always suggesting that we need certain products, but do you really need all of them? We use so many cosmetics and toiletries—like hair spray, nail polish, shaving cream, soap, shampoo, and deodorant—which also means a lot of associated packaging and waste. When choosing your cosmetics and toiletries, find products that not only are natural and organic, but also have minimal, recyclable, or biodegradable packaging. Only buy what you need, and invest in high-quality, classic cosmetics and colors for your blush, eye shadow, and lipstick that will outlast short-lived fads and fashion trends. And always remember to recycle your containers whenever you can.

• *you don't need a multitude of products to be clean and beautiful*

Photo: Corbis Australia

something fragranced

62

The next time you purchase an off-the-shelf beauty product, check the contents for potentially harmful industrial chemical compounds called phthalates. Virtually everything in your bathroom cupboard or cosmetics bag can contain them, including fragrances, shampoo, conditioner, aftershave, body gels, hair spray, and deodorant. Mounting scientific evidence demonstrates that exposure to phthalates may have serious health implications. Also, fragranced chemicals are the number one cause of allergic reactions, and the volatile organic chemicals (VOCs) emitted by fragrance products can contribute to poor indoor air quality. There *are* alternatives. Actively research and choose products that don't contain phthalates or VOC-laden fragrances. You'll feel and look better for it.

• *employ a fragrance-free policy and breathe easier*

Photo: Corbis Australia

63

free health care

The average home and workplace is host to a staggering array of chemicals and toxins, yet the health benefits of fresh air and natural light are well known—and free. Enjoy the outdoors more by bringing them inside with natural light. Regularly detox your home by opening windows and doors to refresh the air, and install skylights to enjoy natural light for up to 14 hours a day. Invest in air-purifying houseplants such as a peace lily, Boston fern, or spider plant. Choose heating and cooling systems that circulate fresh air instead of systems that recirculate old air through your home or workplace.

• *indulge in fresh air and natural light*

Photo: Corbis Australia

antibacterial soap

Those pump-bottle antibacterial hand washes were once only seen in hospitals, but now they're an everyday item in the home. There are growing environmental and health concerns that the overuse of hand washes with antimicrobial (germ-killing) properties may even encourage the development of resistant bacteria, or superbugs. In addition, there's no conclusive evidence that these antibacterial products have any better germ-fighting properties than plain old soap and water. The Centers for Disease Control and Prevention (CDC) advocates a 20-second wash with soap and water as the most effective way to clean your hands and to avoid spreading germs. It might even be more prudent, and better for the environment, if you stick with an eco-friendly bar of soap to prevent more chemicals from being washed down the drain and into our waterways.

• *avoid overusing antibacterial products*

Whether in your own backyard or in a faraway country, forests and trees are critical to the well-being of the entire planet. Absorbing carbon dioxide, providing shade, and preventing erosion are just a few ways they protect the earth. To keep trees and forests abundant and healthy, plant new trees in your neighborhood and actively support larger reforestation projects.

your backyard

65

respect rain forests

Increasing land development and the burgeoning human population currently threaten rain forests all over the world; every second, an area of rain forest the size of a football field disappears. Rain forests cover only 7 percent of Earth's land, but they contain half of its flora and fauna. Generating about 40 percent of the world's oxygen, rain forests are not only Earth's lungs, but also the world's largest gardens. Pumping vital oxygen into the atmosphere, they are home to thousands of different birds, mammals, insects, and plants. Support campaigns to preserve and help protect our rain forests from logging and economic exploitation.

• *let's treat the earth's remaining rain forests with greater respect*

Photo: Marian Kyte

plant for the planet

66

In the past 400 years, 90 percent of the old-growth forests that once grew in the continental United States have been eradicated. Much of the virgin forests that remain are on public property, but they're still endangered. In the Pacific Northwest, for example, some 80 percent of the forest is scheduled to be felled. Since deforestation accounts for 15 to 20 percent of annual global greenhouse gas emissions, reducing the cutting of trees and planting more can help. Restore the tree population in your community by joining the Billion Tree Campaign, the United Nations Environment Programme's worldwide tree planting campaign. The campaign aims to plant at least one billion trees worldwide every year. The average tree produces approximately 260 pounds of oxygen per year and can remove as much CO_2 in a year as that produced by a car driving 26,000 miles.

• *help to plant a billion trees each year*

Photo: Marian Kyte

a cool house

One of the most efficient ways to keep your home cool isn't even *in* the house! Trees and plants that provide shade can significantly reduce the heat that penetrates your home, so carefully planted trees and shrubs in the right locations can reduce the intensity of the sun. Properly placed deciduous trees will also help you enjoy the sun's warmth in winter and offer protective shade in summer. New plants lower greenhouse gas emissions and provide habitats for wildlife, and they can also lower cooling costs by up to 75 percent.

• **use plants and trees wisely to lower your energy bills**

Photo: Corbis Australia

a potted garden

It doesn't matter how much space you have at home—with the right care, just about anything can thrive in pots. Grow some flowers to brighten things up—sunflowers look wonderful and are easy to grow—or plant a cactus garden that needs little water. Native plants are great for attracting birds and are increasingly popular because of their drought tolerance. There are a number of hybrid plant varieties now available, with improved floral characteristics and hardiness. You can also decorate your garden with painted rocks and pebbles or make signs for plants and herbs using Popsicle sticks; paint the signs bright colors to create a brighter and more interesting garden.

• *bring your garden to life with native plants*

Photo: Corbis Australia

bio-diversified backyard

69

Nature finds its balance in a complex network of mutual dependence. Each species provides benefits to other flora and fauna. A tree might feed one animal and shelter another. In a mature forest, there are several main layers of vegetation in which different animals live. Replicate this in your garden by combining tall trees like oaks, pines, or hemlocks with smaller trees and tall shrubs such as dogwood, almond, redwood, and evergreens. Also consider bushy and berry-yielding shrubs such as holly or pyracantha. Use grasses, sedge, and creepers like ivies for groundcover and a layer of wildflowers, herbs, or ferns, followed by mulch or leaf matter, fallen branches, logs, and rocks. Substitute terra-cotta pipes for hollow logs to give small rodents and amphibians a place to hide from predators. Selecting trees and plants that are indigenous to your area will be more helpful to wildlife and to your landscape.

• *create a haven for native wildlife*

Photo: Marian Kyte
Inset: Corbis Australia

bird life

Birds bring life to a garden by adding color, valuable fertilizer, and pest control. With just 3.6 percent of the U.S. landmass reserved for national parks, neighborhood gardens are valuable potential habitats. Birds like taller trees for roosting and nesting, shrubs for flowers and fruits, and clearings to hunt for seeds and insects. Hollow logs or birdhouses, as well as a freshwater supply, will put more feathers in your cap. So will keeping your yard predator free; if you have a cat, put a bell on its collar and keep it inside at night. Provide freshwater with a birdbath or pond, and plant indigenous plants for a natural food source.

• *make your garden a bird habitat*

banish the weeds

71

Many of our gardens feature non-native plants, which, if they thrive, may become invasive, spreading from your yard or garden with serious consequences for other native plants. These invaders can threaten endangered plant and animal species, agriculture, pastoral industries, and even tourism when they wipe out indigenous species in parks and waterways. In California, the eucalyptus tree (originally imported from its native Australia for lumber) has spread so rapidly that it has crowded out native plants, consumes huge amounts of water, and has proven nearly impossible to eradicate. Ask your local nursery or garden store for a list of indigenous plants, and restore the natural habitat at home. Seek out community initiatives that strive to clear local roadways and parks of invasive weeds and restore the native plant populations in your area.

• *keep your garden local*

Photo: Marian Kyte

use the landscape

72

When planning water as a feature of your garden and landscape, keep water efficiency in mind. Make the most of water running off sloping, rocky, and paved areas by bordering them with plant beds. Create depressions or ponds where water can collect to seep back into the ground and replenish the water table, rather than sending it down the storm-water drain. A pond is a valuable addition to a garden ecosystem, as it attracts birds and frogs. With the right plantings, a pond will provide a habitat for native frogs that will eat mosquitoes, other insects, and algae. Or consider xeriscape, a popular landscaping concept that conserves water.

• *create a healthier garden by working with the landscape*

Photo: Corbis Australia

73

home grown

No matter what size your garden is—a balcony or a quarter-acre block—you can grow your own 100 percent organic produce. Organic gardening produces healthy plants with high nutrient levels, reduces potential health risks, provides healthy habitats, and protects soil and water quality. Remember that the key to a robust, productive garden is its soil. If your plants have rich soil and water, they should be able to withstand most insects. However, if you do have insects, always opt for natural alternatives to insecticides—for example, plant garlic, onions, or marigolds to keep aphids, flies, and caterpillars away. Start with the basics to provide a regular source of your favorite produce, like tomatoes, salad greens, basil, strawberries, and cucumbers.

• *enjoy your very own organic produce*

Photo: Corbis Australia

74

chicken little

If you have the space, keeping a couple of chickens in your backyard will provide a great source of fresh, free-range eggs. Letting your chickens out to roam for a few hours a day will help keep garden pests, such as caterpillars and slugs, at bay. Each chick also generates around 220 pounds of superb organic fertilizer every year. Grab some two-by-fours and a roll of chicken wire, and spend a weekend with the kids building the family a chicken coop; you'll find there are plenty of building plans on the Web. First, however, check with your local town council for regulations and advice on keeping chickens.

• *discover the benefits of chickens in your backyard*

Photo: Corbis Australia

worm your way in

Employ the world's best recycling specialist: the humble worm. You can establish a thriving worm farm in an unused corner of your yard, with a few modified stackable crates, some compost and newspaper, and some worms from your local nursery or garden shop. Worms dig upward to fresher food scraps, and the debris they leave behind makes fertilizer for your vegetable garden. It doesn't take long for the worms to reduce food scraps, paper, dirt, and hair into a pile of castings and liquid (it's really worm pee!). Make sure you keep the worm farm moist at all times, and don't feed them onions, garlic, or citrus scraps—they're too acidic—or your worms will leave the farm!

- *turn half your garbage into compost*

Illustration: Marian Kyte

gray is the new blue

Photo: Corbis Australia

You can recycle water for non-potable (non-drinking) purposes with a readily available graywater recycling system. Graywater—all non-toilet household wastewater from baths, showers, washing machines, and sinks—can be redirected, filtered, and treated for other domestic uses, such as flushing the toilet. A graywater system can be anything from a bucket in the shower or a tank collecting laundry water to a comprehensive system using plants and microorganisms to treat water from all household outlets. Remember that only about half the water used by the average household needs to be of crystal-clear drinking quality. Consult your plumber or local town officials about state and federal government regulations, tax credits or rebates, and health and safety issues.

• *lower your demand on the water supply*

don't mow it away

77

Powered lawn equipment can be a big enemy of the environment, not to mention the associated noise pollution it can create. One gas-powered lawn mower generates 11 times the air pollution that a new car does for every hour of operation. According to the EPA, Americans use a staggering 800 million gallons of gas each year cutting their lawns, so that's an enormous amount of CO_2 emissions escaping into the atmosphere. Add to that the EPA's statistic that over 17 million gallons of fuel are spilled each year while people refuel lawn and garden equipment. If you have a small lawn, opt for a manual mower. Electric mowers are fine for a smaller suburban yard. Eliminating fuel-powered mowers, leaf blowers, weed whackers, and trimmers (in favor of rakes, manual edgers, and brooms) would greatly reduce air pollution and groundwater contamination.

• *swap garden gas-guzzlers for eco-efficient alternatives*

Photo: Corbis Australia

cover up

Nearly one-third of all U.S. residential water goes to watering lawns and landscapes—more in the summer—which amounts to over 7.5 billion gallons each day! Native plants and ground covers need less water, so consider an indigenous garden that will lower your water bill. By surrounding your garden and flower beds with mulch, you can cut water loss through evaporation by up to 70 percent and reduce your water needs by up to 50 percent. Mulch also limits weed growth and prevents air-borne garden diseases. Pine bark mulch can even be used for children's play areas; it is just as safe as grass and doesn't require watering.

• ***plant and mulch to lower your water consumption***

Photo: Corbis Australia

Work with the planet, not against it. Take a walk outside and look at what Mother Nature has to share: Go surfing, fishing, swimming, running, sailing, hiking, biking, skiing, or climbing. The more time you spend outdoors, the more you'll appreciate the natural environment and want to protect and preserve it.

enjoyment

79

enjoy your
world

Whether or not you have a dog to walk, you can always get out and enjoy the great outdoors. The world is always changing—keep an eye on your favorite places and watch how they change with the seasons. Are the trees evergreens, or do they lose their leaves in winter and burst into flower in spring? Many parts of the United States have only one or two main seasons, so it seems as if your outdoor world remains pretty much the same year-round—but if you look closely, you will notice subtle changes throughout the year. Even people living in cities have access to parks, so wherever you live and whatever your climate, find an outdoor spot that makes you feel good and enjoy your world.

• *appreciate the natural world on your doorstep*

Photo: Corbis Australia

turn up the volume

Support outdoor events that are clean and green. Nationally known music festivals like Bonnaroo (held annually in Manchester, Tennessee) and Bumbershoot (held in Seattle, Washington) are committed to spreading the word about environmental awareness, promoting messages such as "Buy Local," banning the use of Styrofoam at their concerts, composting, recycling, and planting a community vegetable garden on concert grounds. Parts of the music industry are becoming powerful green activists. The Live Earth concerts in 2007, which were held around the world, focused people on the future of the planet and the need to combat climate change. Many classical composers wrote their greatest works in response to nature and the world around them—such as Beethoven's *Pastoral Symphony* and Vivaldi's *Four Seasons*. Listen to music and support musicians and events that inspire you to make a difference!

• *find inspiration in a song—participate in green events*

get creative

81

Entertainment doesn't have to be an electronic or economic transaction; you can make your own entertainment and fun. A lot of what we throw out can be recycled into gifts, cards, fun activities, or decorations. There's nothing quite like making papier-mâché with kids to recycle old newspaper. Get creative with old cardboard boxes and make forts, castles, and trains. You are only limited by your imagination. Puppets, masks, mobiles, collages, mosaics, musical instruments, and hand-made birthday cards are all things that can be made from reused and recycled household materials. Get creative and entertain yourself!

• *unleash your creative spirit and recycle*

Photo: Marian Kyte

faded
TV stars

With 2.6 televisions per U.S. household and major advances in technology, your TV has become a chief culprit of greenhouse gas emissions—right behind refrigerators, space heaters and coolers, and water heaters. The energy efficiency of TVs and other home electronics is now being assessed through the Energy Star rating program to help you make the greenest choice. So make sure that when it's time to purchase your new, state-of-the-art plasma or LCD wide-screen TV, you choose an Energy Star–qualified model. If all the electronics in U.S. homes were replaced with Energy Star–rated models, more than 25 billion pounds of greenhouse gas emissions would be prevented—the amount produced by more than two million cars.

• *choose the greener television*

Photo: Corbis Australia

83

get on your bike

Get into cycling—it's cheap, eco-efficient, good for your health, and fun. Transportation emissions—which account for one-third of U.S. greenhouse gas emissions—are rising faster than emissions from any other sector. Our lifestyles are built around using our cars to get to work, to buy the groceries, to drop the kids off at school, to pick up fast food, and to go shopping at the mall. Half of all car trips are less than three miles—a distance that can be covered just as quickly on a bike, taking traffic and parking into account. Choose two wheels over four; there are real health benefits to be gained, for you and the earth.

- *commit to exchanging your car for your bike at least once a week*

Photo: Corbis Australia

play fair

Sports are among life's great pleasures. But make sure your sports equipment consists of certified Fair Trade products made with sustainable, exploitation-free practices. Whatever your sport, there are Fair Trade balls available (meeting all official game standards) as well as apparel. You can hit the greens with degradable golf tees and play fair with water-soluble and recycled soccer balls, footballs, basketballs, and more. Support the mission of the Global Sports Alliance (GSA): to leave a healthy environment for future generations through initiatives like Sports-Eco.Net, which promotes the recycling and reuse of sports equipment in developing countries. You can also allocate part or all of your earnings from your eBay sales to GSA.

• *your equipment should be socially responsible, too*

Illustration: Marian Kyte

waterworld

There's one sure way to find out just how magical our planet is: Experience its natural wonders for ourselves. The United States has thousands of miles of coastline, so you may be able to spot a wide range of fish, whales, dolphins, and even manatees. Dolphins are especially friendly and intelligent mammals and have been much loved by humans for centuries. Unfortunately, their survival, along with that of manatees, is threatened, so learn how to treat them properly. Whale- and dolphin-watching trips are a good way to learn more about marine life. For example, look for migrating whales from high points on the East and West Coasts from June to November (whales along U.S. coasts migrate north to feed and south to give birth).

• *discover the natural wonders in our oceans*

Photos: (top) Lady Elliot Island, Tourism Queensland; (below) Monkey Mia, Tourism Western Australia

86

fish and chips

Fishing is one of the world's favorite pastimes, and seafood is an important part of a healthy diet. We shouldn't assume that the vast numbers of fish in the ocean will be there forever, though; many are seriously endangered. Fish along U.S. coastlines—such as New England cod, West Coast rockfish, and bluefin tuna—are under increasing threat, due to the $16 billion in annual seafood sales at U.S. supermarkets and commercial overfishing. So whether you catch your own or buy from the fish store, make sure you avoid species that are underprotected or under threat. Check with local fish and wildlife authorities for information on protected species, catch-and-release and minimum size regulations, and possession limits. Always treat fish humanely and protect their environment. Don't leave your trash behind—broken lines, hooks, plastic bait bags, and plastic bottles pollute waterways and harm aquatic life. And when purchasing fish, make choices that support responsible, sustainable fishing practices.

- *support sustainable fishing at the beach and at the dinner table*

pristine wilderness

The original inhabitants of North America lived in harmony with the land for thousands of years. Many of them still do, and it is a privilege to be allowed to experience this great country with them. The United States has 58 national parks and 120 historic parks and historic sites. More than 84 million acres of land is managed by the National Park Service—about 3.6 percent of U.S. land areas. Even more of the nation's wild lands, including state forests, nature parks, and conservation reserves, are protected and managed by state and local governments as well as other organizations. If you visit a national park, take great care not to pollute or damage the land, to respect the wildlife you encounter, and to enjoy the great outdoors!

• *explore your national parks—discover the fragility our environment*

Photo: Geir Olav Lyngfjell/Shutterstock

88

protect the reefs

Colorful coral reefs are unique ecosystems that are home to a wide array of aquatic plants and animals. But many of the world's reefs—from Australia to the Hawaiian Islands to the Maldives—are in decline. In the next ten years, it is estimated that 30 percent of coral reefs will be destroyed or seriously damaged. Reef degradation is caused by climate change, ocean acidification, overfishing, pollution, and even increased tourism (when more people visit the reefs, more corals are broken, collected, or accidentally damaged). Like so many natural environments sensitive to temperature changes and pollution, the reefs will benefit from every environmentally friendly thing you do, including reducing your contribution to global warming. Another option: Get involved in direct coral reef monitoring initiatives, such as the Coral Reef Alliance.

• *become aware of what you can do to help protect coral reefs*

Photo: Lady Elliot Island, Tourism Queensland

byo
(and take it with you)

So much of the American lifestyle is about sharing good food with friends and family in the great outdoors—but make sure your next outing or picnic at the park is environmentally sustainable, too. Pack a homemade picnic lunch instead of buying overpackaged supermarket food. Revive the Thermos of freshly made tea, coffee, or hot chocolate. Avoid disposable fast-food containers. Fill your own water bottles instead of buying plastic ones. Opt out of extras such as wooden chopsticks, napkins, and plastic utensils when possible. And remember to keep America beautiful—protect and conserve our natural environment.

• packing a homemade picnic can preserve and protect the environment

Photo: Marian Kyte

90

appreciate the wild

Photo: Marian Kyte

Some places are so special that they are put on heritage lists to protect and preserve them. As of 2009, the United States had 20 World Heritage Sites recognized by UNESCO, including 12 national parks. Among them is the spectacular Grand Canyon National Park in Arizona, considered one of the seven natural wonders of the world. There are also giant redwood trees—the tallest trees on the planet—in forests along the California coast at Redwood National Park, and two of the world's most active volcanoes, Mauna Loa and Kilauea, at Hawaii Volcanoes National Park.

• *support and enjoy the best of the world's natural wild places*

The United States is the world's biggest producer of waste per capita. In 2007, it created 254 million tons of trash, of which only one-quarter was recycled. The United States also emits more CO_2 from burning fossil fuels than any other country. As the insatiable desire for new products increases, it continues to make unsustainable demands on Earth's finite resources.

action

what's your plan for the planet?

91

W e all know that our modern lifestyle is jeopardizing the future of our planet, but what can we do? Well, a lot—you just need a plan! We plan for our retirement, our holidays, and even our weekends, so why not plan to lead a more sustainable life? Change your behavior to think climate-friendly and low-carbon instead of convenient and disposable. History is full of individuals whose talent, vision, and commitment have made the world a better place. You, too, can make a difference. Make a decision to be part of the solution and be true green for a carbon-neutral future.

• *make a plan to become carbon neutral*

Photo: Corbis Australia

best foot forward

Everything you do, use, buy, and consume in your daily life has the capacity to reduce or contribute to global warming. Your carbon footprint is a measure of the adverse impact your activities have on the environment; it represents the amount of CO_2 your lifestyle contributes to global warming. The level of CO_2 emissions per person in the United States is among the highest in the world—each American creates more than 21.5 tons of carbon emissions every year. In the time it takes you to read this paragraph, Americans will have generated more than 8,200 tons of carbon emissions! Help to reverse this trend by taking responsibility for your (and your household's) emissions. Regularly measure your footprint by using one of the many available carbon emissions calculators. Actively practice the principles of the "5 Rs"—Rethink, Reduce, Reuse, Repair, and Recycle—to reduce your emissions and your footprint.

• *know your footprint and reduce it*

Illustration: Marian Kyte

rethink and reduce

Houses, cars, appliances, accessories . . . as our insatiable desire for new things increases, we continue to make unsustainable demands on Earth's finite resources. We need to rethink and reduce our consumption of non-essentials and reduce our levels of personal waste. The United States is among the world's highest producers of trash. The average American generates 4.6 pounds of waste every day, and most of it goes straight into landfills. So think before you buy. Do you really need it? Is there a greener alternative? Don't assume that what you throw away is disposable or biodegradable. These small acts of awareness may seem insignificant, but collectively they add up. Make the necessary change from living a consumer lifestyle to living a sustainable lifestyle.

• *stop wasting non-renewable resources*

Photo: Corbis Australia

94

Photo: Corbis Australia

reuse
and repair

So much of what we use in everyday life is not disposable. We anecdotally refer to bags, pens, diapers, and batteries as disposable when in reality, they are far from it. Each year Americans throw away a staggering 100 billion new plastic shopping bags and 180,000 tons of household batteries, many of which will remain in the environment. In fact, most of what we consume ends up as garbage within months, weeks, days, or even minutes. Before you buy, upgrade, dispose of, or replace an item, ask yourself if it can be saved, used for something else, or repaired to extend its usefulness.

• *think renewable and degradable*

less is more

95

The United States is the biggest consumer nation in the world. The average American shops for 24 minutes each day, which adds up to $4 trillion—and colossal amounts of waste. Every day, advertisements encourage us to equate quality of life with consumption. But every item you buy contains embodied energy, water, and waste in its production, transport, and disposal. Some may say retail therapy is good for you, but our levels of consumer spending and consumption are unsustainable—and are costing our planet. Before any purchase, ask yourself if you really need it. In most cases, your life won't be any worse without it. Achieving a sustainable lifestyle means buying a bit less of everything. Try setting aside a day to be Buy Nothing Day.

• *shop for only what you need*

Photo: Corbis Australia

share and share alike

We all learn to share as children, and we shouldn't stop as we grow up. Sharing builds relationships and communities, and it can reduce your ecological footprint, too. Share your tools, your toys (including grown-up ones), your time, and even your home. The growth in single-person households is the single greatest contributor to increasing levels of household carbon emissions. Many of our elderly citizens are living alone, which means they use more energy and resources than if they lived with their adult children or extended families. A single-person household produces double the waste of someone sharing with three others. Single-person households also waste resources with the unnecessary duplication of household goods and appliances. Think of ways you can share resources within your own neighborhood, such as the lawn mower, garden tools, or fresh produce from your garden. Carpool to school, to the local train station, or to work.

• ***share the planet's resources and reduce waste***

Photo: Marian Kyte

show a cooperative spirit

local markets | organic food | fresh produce

Cooperatives can be found in many walks of life, from organic farmers' markets and utility cooperatives to housing collectives, credit unions, pension funds, community radio stations, and Internet service providers. These businesses pool assets for the shared gain of their members and create local investment, services, and jobs. Whatever profits they make are more likely to be invested back into the local community and on less wasteful consumption. Cooperatives can also create products and services that other companies might not regard as profitable enough, thus building a market for more sustainable business practices. Four in ten Americans—some 120 million people—are members of local cooperatives. Come on board!

• *support your local economy and sustainable businesses*

Illustration: Marian Kyte

the power of one

98

You might be cynical about politicians, but don't be cynical about the power of your vote and the importance of your participation in the democratic process. The power of one vote can change the course of history. One vote changed France from a monarchy to a republic in 1875, and one vote decided that Americans would speak English rather than German in 1776. Local, state, and federal governments make the big decisions about the type of world we live in. Register to vote, and don't miss your opportunity to have your say about who should set the agenda, now and in the future.

- **use your vote and keep the environment on the political agenda**

Vote!

1 for the planet

become a 99
green leader

If you're frustrated by inaction on climate change in your local community, workplace, or school, take the lead and become a green leader. You can start a tree-planting or water-conservation group in your neighborhood, initiate a recycling program in your workplace, or even run for your town council. Even just by campaigning on a local environmental issue, you can raise awareness of an important community cause and, if elected, as a town council member you will be part of the legislative process of strategic planning for the future of your community.

• *be proactive—become a positive force for change*

Illustration: Marian Kyte

be energy efficient every day

100

Photo: Corbis Australia

One of the simplest and most effective things you can do to address climate change is to become energy efficient in all aspects of your life. Start by switching to renewable energy and always switching off unused lights. Earth Hour, run by the World Wildlife Fund, is an initiative that calls on individuals and businesses to turn off their lights for one hour of one day once a year. Earth Hour 2008 united more than 50 million people across seven continents, which demonstrated our power to do something about our planet's future. It was the biggest voluntary power-down in history. By being energy efficient and making small changes every day, not just during Earth Hour, we can each do our part.

• *show you care with one simple action*

websites

websites

TRAVEL		
Responsible Tourism	Green Passport	greenpassport.us
Destinations	UNESCO World Heritage Site	whc.unesco.org
	Visit National Parks	nps.gov
Companies	Earth Dive—Global Dive Log	earthdive.com
	Ethical Traveler	ethicaltraveler.org
	Green Globe—For Communities and Organizations	greenglobe.org
	Lonely Planet	lonelyplanet.com
	Nature Conservancy Travel	nature.org/aboutus/travel
	Practical Ecotourism	planeta.com
	Responsible Travel	responsibletravel.com
	Sustainable Travel International	sustainabletravelinternational.org
Slow Travel	Amtrak	amtrak.com
	Eurostar	eurostar.com
	Great Rail Journeys—Worldwide	greatrail.com
	Great Southern Rail—Australia	gsr.com.au
	The Man in Seat Sixty-One	seat61.com
	Online Slow Travel Community	slowtrav.com
	Orient-Express Train Travel	orient-expresstrains.com
	Rocky Mountaineer Vacations—Canada	rockymountaineer.com
	Slow Travel and More	slowtravel.com
	Slow Travel Info	slowmovement.com
	Slow Travel Tours	slowtraveltours.com
Travel Calculators	Carbon Footprint	carbonfund.org
	Ecological Footprint	myfootprint.org
	Ecological Footprint Calculator	footprintnetwork.org/en/index.php/GFN/page/calculators
	Energy Calculator	eere.energy.gov/calculators

Offsetting	Carbon Offsets	climatecare.com
	Living Smart—Carbon Offsets and More	terrapass.com
Airports/Customs	Chicago O'Hare Airport	ohare.com
	JFK Airport	panynj.gov/aviation/jfkframe.htm
	Los Angeles World Airports	lawa.org
	Miami Airport	miami-airport.com
	U.S. Customs	customs.gov

CELEBRATIONS

Occasions	Arbor Day	arborday.org
	Clean Up the World Day	cleanuptheworld.org
	Earth Day	earthday.net
	Earth Hour	earthhourus.org
	World Habitat Day	unhabitat.org/categories.asp?catid=588
Calendar Events	Fair Trade Chocolates	organicconsumers.org/valentines/index.cfm
	Holiday Crafts with Recycled Goods	allfreecrafts.com/recycling-crafts/index.shtml
	Valentine's Day	holidays.kaboose.com/valentines-day
Green Weddings	Conflict-Free Diamonds	conflictfreediamonds.org
	Go Green Weddings	planetgreen.discovery.com/go-green/ weddings
	Green Elegance Weddings	greeneleganceweddings.com
	Green Wedding Guide	thegreenbrideguide.com
	Green Wedding Jewelry	greenkarat.com
Eco-Gifts	Charitable Gifts	heifer.org
	EarthTech Products	earthtechproducts.com
	EcoExpress Gifts	ecoexpress.com
	Fair Trade Products	globalexchangestore.org
	Fish Lips Paper Designs	fishlipspaperdesigns.com
	Gifts from Recycled Materials	eco-artware.com
	Green Gift Guide	greengiftguide.com
	Oxfam America Unwrapped	oxfamamericaunwrapped.com
	World Vision—Useful Gifts	worldvision.org/GiftCatalog
Green Party Needs	Danny Seo	dannyseo.com
	Green Party Goods	greenpartygoods.com

Green Party Supplies   greenpartysupply.com
Heritage Turkey Foundation   heritageturkeyfoundation.org
Slow Food USA   slowfoodusa.org

FAMILY AND HEALTH

Food	Eartheasy	eartheasy.com/eat_menu.htm
	Equal Exchange	equalexchange.com
	Fair Trade Products	transfairusa.org
	Go Meat Free	priceofmeat.com
	Green Restaurant Association	dinegreen.com
	Living and Raw Foods	living-foods.com
	Organic Dairy Farming	cornucopia.org
	Organic Farming	localharvest.org
	Papa's Organics Food	papasorganic.com
	Rwanda Coffee Growers	spreadproject.org/home.php
	Seafood Choices Alliance	seafoodchoices.com
	Slow Food USA	slowfoodusa.com
	Sustainable Seafood Guide	montereybayaquarium.org/cr/seafoodwatch.aspx
	Sustainable Table	sustainabletable.org
	Vegetarian Lifestyle	goveg.com
Organic Products	All About Organic	organic.org
	Bedding, Linens	kushtush.com
	Hemp, Organic Clothing	rawganique.com
	Natural Alternatives to Pesticides	kidsorganics.com/Alternatives%20to%20Toxins.htm
Eco-funerals	Eco-funeral Planning	backyardnature.com/cgi-bin/gt/tpl.h,content=573
	Recycled Cardboard Caskets	eeternity.com/index.htm
Green Baby	Children's Health Environmental Coalition	healthychild.org
	Eco-Friendly Pregnancy Tips	thecradle.com/eco-friendly-tips-and-advice-for-pregnancy-and-baby
	Green Baby Guide	greenbabyguide.com
	Munchskins—Skin Care Products	baby-skin-care.info
	Wee Generation	seventhgeneration.com/Natural-Baby

Pets	Caring for Pets	pbskids.org/itsmylife/family/pets
	EarthAnimal	earthanimal.com
	Eco-Pet	ecopetlife.com
	How to Build a Frog Pond	frogsvilleusa.com/how-to/frog-pond.html
Water Conservation	American Water Works Association	drinktap.org
	Water Info for Kids	drinktap.org/kidsdnn
	Water Saver Home	h2ouse.net
	WaterSense	epa.gov/watersense
	Water Use It Wisely	wateruseitwisely.com
Energy-wise	Alliance to Save Energy	ase.org/consumers
	Clean Electricity	wecansolveit.org
	Energy Savers	energysavers.gov
	Your Home—A Consumer's Guide to Energy	eere.energy.gov/consumer/your_home
Certification	Energy Star Rating System	energystar.gov
	Fair Trade Federation	fairetradefeferation.org
	Forest Stewardship Council	fscus.org
	NSF International Certification System	nfs.org
	Organic Trade Association	ota.com
	U.S. Green Building Council	usgbc.org
	USA Made Products	stillmadeinusa.com
	Water Quality Association	wqa.org
Around the House	Clean Air Gardening	cleanairgardening.com/houseplants.html
	Eliminating PVC in Your Home	watoxics.org/files/vinyl.pdf
	Federal Tax Credits	energystar.gov/taxcredits
	A Green Home Renovator's Guide	care2.com/greenliving/a-green-home-renovators-guide-part-1.html
	Green Living	greenlivingonline.com
	Greener Choices—Products for a Better Planet	greenerchoices.org
	Rechargeable Batteries	greenbatteries.com
Home Design	Built-e, Eco-Friendly Houses	built-e.com
	Forest Certification Resource Center	certifiedwood.org
	Environmental Home Center	environmentalhomecenter.com
	GreenHomeGuide	greenhomeguide.com

	Green Insulation	therenewableplanet.com/green/ reduceenergy/energy-efficient-insulation.aspx
	Passive Solar Home Design	energysavers.gov/your_home/designing_ remodeling/index.cfm/mytopic=10250
Campaigns	Buy Nothing Day	adbusters.org/campaigns/bnd
	The Campaign for Safe Cosmetics	safecosmetics.org
	Donate Used Eyeglasses	eyeseemission.org
	Health Care Without Harm	noharm.org
	Mercury-Free Health Care	mercuryfreehealthcare.org
	Stop Junk Mail	mailstopper.tonic.com
	Unite for Sight	uniteforsight.org
	U.S. EPA—Mercury Info, News	epa.gov/mercury
Cosmetics	Chemicals in Cosmetics	thegreenguide.com/health-safety/dirty- dozen-decoder
	Eco-Friendly Cosmetics	greenzer.com/eco-friendly-cosmetics_7_g
	Green Your . . . Cosmetics	greenyour.com/body/cosmetics
	No Shampoo Challenge	noshampoo.org
	Personal Care Products "Skin Deep" Database	cosmeticsdatabase.com
	Saffron Rouge	saffronrouge.com
Shopping	Green Products	ecofabulous.com
	One Percent for the Planet	onepercentfortheplanet.org
	Product Ratings	goodguide.com
	Responsible Shopper	responsibleshopper.org
	Reusable Shopping Bags	reusablebags.com

YOUR BACKYARD

Greenery	Citizen Forestry	treepeople.org
	Cooling a House with Shrubs and Trees	house-energy.com/Shadow/House-Trees- Shrubs.htm
	Gardener's Guide to Global Warming	nwf.org/gardenersguide
	Green Roofs	greenroofs.com
	Native Plant Landscapes	plantnative.org
	Sustainable Gardening Blog	sustainablegardeningblog.com
	Trees for the Future	treesftf.org
	UNEP Billion Tree Campaign	unep.org/billiontreecampaign

In the Backyard	All About Compost	epa.gov/epawaste/conserve/rrr/composting/index.htm
	Attracting Birds and Butterflies to Your Garden	howtoattractbirds.com
	Backyard Conservation	nrcs.usda.gov/feature/backyard
	Composting	compostguide.com
	Eco-Gardening Blog	site.cleanairgardening.com/info
	People Powered Machines	peoplepoweredmachines.com
	Raising Chickens	poultryone.com
	Sustainable Gardening	sustainable-gardening.com
	Xeriscaping ABCs	howstuffworks.com/lawn-garden/professional-landscaping/alternative-methods/xeriscaping3.htm
Water Usage	Clean Up Our Water	nrdc.org/water/pollution/gsteps.asp
	Earth Easy	eartheasy.com/grow_menu.htm
	Natural Lawn Care	savingwater.org/docs/natlawncare.pdf
	Saving Water in the Garden	greenlivingtips.com/articles/242/1/Saving-water-in-the-garden.html
	Xeriscape Design	wateruseitwisely.com/100-ways-to-conserve/outdoor-tips/how-to/landscape-to-xeriscape/index.php

ENJOYMENT

Outdoors	America on the Move	aom3.americaonthemove.org
	Appalachian Mountain Club	outdoors.org
	Dolphin Research	dolphins.org
	Ecotourism	ecotourism.org
	Everglades National Park	nps.gov/ever/index.htm
	Fair Trade Sports	fairtradesports.com
	Go Camping America	gocampingamerica.com
	The Grand Canyon	nps.gov/grca/index.htm
	Hawai'i Volcanoes National Park	nps.gov/havo
	NASA—Earth Topics	nasa.gov/topics/earth/index.html
	National Parks Conservation Association	npca.org
	National Seashores	usparks.about.com/blparktypes-ns.htm
	Sports-Eco.net	sports-eco.net/ENGLISH/2index_en.html

Support/Share	Baby/Child Rental Equipment	deliciousbaby.com/journal/2008/jul/27/safety-tips-renting-carseat
	Clothing, Book, and Toy Exchanges	stretcher.com/stories/00/000124a.cfm
	Clothing Swaps	clothingswaps.com
	Neighborhood Tool Sharing	centerforsustainableliving.org/library/?p=14
	Toy Libraries	ecochildsplay.com/2009/01/25/free-toys-and-less-clutter-sharing-the-toy-library-love

ACTION

Education	11th Hour Action	11thhouraction.com
	Beyond Pesticides	beyondpesticides.org/about/mission.htm
	Clean Air, Cool Planet	cleanair-coolplanet.org
	Contact Your U.S. Congressman	congress.org
	Contact Your U.S. Senator	senate.gov
	EPA—Climate Change	epa.gov/climatechange
	Fight Global Warming	fightglobalwarming.com
	An Inconvenient Truth	climatecrisis.net
	National Geographic	nationalgeographic.com/environment
	Plant a Billion Trees	plantabillion.org
	Rainforest Action Network	ran.org
	True Green	betruegreen.com
	Virtual March—Stop Global Warming	stopglobalwarming.org
	Yahoo! Green Take Action Pledge	green.yahoo.com/pledge

Carbon Neutral	Carbon Audits and Offsets	carbonplanet.com
	Carbon Reduction Programs	nativeenergy.com
	Real-Time CO_2 Emissions by Country	breathingearth.net
	Zero Footprint Carbon Calculator	earthhour.zerofootprint.net

Waste/Recycling	Battery Disposal Guide	ehso.com/ehshome/batteries.php
	Cell Phone and Battery Recycling	call2recycle.org
	Collective Good Mobile Phone Recycling	collectivegood.com
	Container Recycling Institute	container-recycling.org
	Electronics Recycling	ecyclingcentral.com
	Internet Consumer Recycling Guide	obviously.com/recycle
	Light Bulb Recycling	lamprecycle.org/
	National Recycling Coalition	nrc-recycle.org
	Paper Recycling	paperrecycles.org
	Recycling Near You	earth911.com

| Recycling Scrap and Waste Materials | recycle.net |
| Solid Waste Facts | learner.org/interactives/garbage/solidwaste. html |

Volunteer and Give	Charity Evaluator	charitynavigator.org
	Clean Up the World	cleanuptheworld.org
	Environmental Volunteer Opportunities	charityguide.org/volunteer/environmental-protection.htm
	The Garden Club of America	gcamerica.org
	Global Volunteers	globalvolunteers.org
	International Coastal Clean-up	oceanconservancy.org
	Keep America Beautiful	kab.org
	The Nature Conservancy	nature.org
	Surfrider Foundation	surfrider.org
	Volunteer Match	volunteermatch.org

Green Groups	Action Network	actionnetwork.org
	American Rivers	americanrivers.org
	Audubon Society	audubon.org
	Center for Food Safety	centerforfoodsafety.org
	Clean Up the World	cleanuptheworld.org
	Environmental Defense Fund— What You Can Do	edf.org/page.cfm?tagID=820
	Environmental Protection Agency	epa.gov
	Environmental Working Group	ewg.org
	Friends of the Earth	foe.org
	Greenpeace	greenpeace.org
	Healthy Child Healthy World	healthychild.org
	National Resources Defense Council— Action Center	nrdc.org/action
	Oceana	oceana.org
	Ocean Conservancy	oceanconservancy.org
	Oxfam America	oxfamamerica.org
	Rainforest Action Network	ran.org
	Rocky Mountain Institute	rmi.org
	Save Our Environment	saveourenvironment.org
	Sierra Club	sierraclub.org
	The Wilderness Society	wilderness.org
	World Wildlife Fund	wwf.org
	Worldwatch Institute	worldwatch.org

Green Investment	*GreenMoney Journal*	greenmoneyjournal.com
	Socially Responsible Investing	socialinvest.org
	Sustainable Business Advice	sustainablebusiness.com
	Sustainable Investing	sustainableinvesting.net
	Wall Street Journal: Environmental Capitol	blogs.wsj.com/environmentalcapital
Green Leaders	Brent Blackwelder	foe.org/brent-blackwelder-president
	Laurie David	lauriedavid.com
	Leonardo DiCaprio	leonardodicaprio.org
	Gloria Flora	s-o-solutions.org/people.html
	Jane Goodall	janegoodall.org
	Al Gore	algore.com
	Richard Heinberg	richardheinberg.com
	Annie Leonard	thestoryofstuff.com
	Bill McKibben	350.org
	Nina Simons	bioneers.org/about/founders
	David Suzuki	davidsuzuki.org
State Agencies	U.S. State Environmental Agencies	epa.gov/epahome/state.htm
Media	David Steinman—Green Patriot Radio	greenpatriot.us
	E/The Environmental Magazine	emagazine.com
	Earth Policy Institute	earth-policy.org
	Environmental Health News	environmentalhealthnews.org
	Environmental Issues Newsletter	environment.about.com
	Environmental News Network	enn.com
	Green Building Resource Guide	greenguide.com
	Green Headlines and Videos	greenenergytv.com
	Green News	planetgreen.discovery.com
	Grist: Environmental News	grist.org
	National Geographic Society	nationalgeographic.com
	No Impact Man	noimpactman.com
	Treehugger	treehugger.com
General Resources	The Daily Green Scoop	thedailygreen.com
	Earth 911	earth911.com
	Eartheasy	eartheasy.com
	Envirolink—Information and News	envirolink.org
	Green Tips	greenglancy.com

	Green Living Guide	greenyour.com
	How Your Elected Officials Vote	vote-smart.org/index.htm
	Mother Earth News	motherearthnews.com
	Organization for Economic Co-operation and Development	oecd.org
	Test Your Environmental IQ	epa.gov/epahome/enviroq
	Tips from the EPA	epa.gov/climatechange/wycd/home.html

Directories/Guides	EcoBusiness Links & Resources	ecobusinesslinks.com
	The Green Guide—National Geographic	thegreenguide.com
	Green Pages	greenamericatoday.org/pubs/greenpages
	Green Search Engine	greenmaven.com
	Green Vehicle Guide	epa.gov/greenvehicles
	Greener Cars Directory	greenercars.org
	U.S. Library Sites	librarysites.info

Community	Green Pages Coop	greenpages.org
	Grocery Coop Directory	cooperativegrocer.coop
	National Coop Directory	coopdirectory.org
	National Cooperative Business Association	ncba.coop

glossary

biodegradable> commonly refers to the process of something breaking down organically into a natural substance (i.e., food scraps can be broken down by worms into compost and used as fertilizer in the garden). *Degradable* refers to something that breaks down and deteriorates chemically. In the case of plastic bags, a biodegradable bag breaks down organically into a natural substance, whereas a degradable bag breaks down only using a chemical additive, often triggered by light or heat.

biodiversity> *bio* means "life," so *biodiversity* means the great variety of living things that exist in a given geographic area. It also refers to the multitude of living organisms on the earth and the differences among them, including species and ecosystems. All life is interconnected, so we must do all that we can to maintain as many species as possible.

biofuel> a safe form of gas or liquid made from renewable or recycled materials that can be used as a fuel. For example, ethanol is made from cereals and sugarcane, and biodiesel is made from vegetable oils (perhaps used in frying foods) or animal waste (like sheep and cattle manure).

bisphenol A > commonly referred to as BPA, this is an organic compound used primarily to make plastics. It is suspected of being hazardous to humans. Low doses of bisphenol A can mimic the body's own hormones, possibly causing negative health effects and creating concern that long-term, low-dose exposure may induce chronic toxicity in humans.

carbon dioxide (CO_2)> a colorless gas that has no smell and is made up of one atom of carbon and two atoms of oxygen. All animals, including humans, breathe out CO_2, and plants absorb it to produce oxygen. It is also produced when fossil fuels are burned to create energy. When too much CO_2 gets trapped in Earth's atmosphere, it causes Earth to heat up.

carbon footprint> a measurement of the amount of greenhouse gas produced by human activities. It is usually measured in tons of carbon dioxide emitted into the atmosphere every year.

carbon neutral> tending to reduce the amount of greenhouse gases humans produce. Examples of carbon-neutral activities are switching to green power, recycling, and walking to school or riding a bicycle instead of driving. You'll still be producing some emissions, so you can choose to "offset" the remainder to become carbon neutral.

carbon offset> a way to make up for some emissions we produce from activities like air travel or driving a car, by supporting renewable energy activities such as programs that invest in solar or wind power, or supporting programs that plant large numbers of trees, which absorb gases like CO_2 and give off oxygen.

carbon sink> a reservoir that can absorb or sequester carbon dioxide from the atmosphere. Trees, the oceans, and soil can all absorb CO_2 and help prevent it from being released back into the atmosphere.

carbon trading> an economic approach to combating pollution caused by greenhouse gases. Companies that release CO_2 into the atmosphere can buy "carbon credits" from organizations that don't, such as tree-planting programs. The aim is to balance the amount of harmful gases being released. The trade costs more for those who release CO_2, while the seller of the carbon credits uses money from the deal to expand their activities and further help the environment. These markets operate like a stock market and are well established in Europe and the United States.

climate change> changes to the overall weather patterns of Earth caused by global warming. This happens when too much CO_2 and other greenhouse gases get into the atmosphere and trap the sun's heat, which normally would be able to escape. It is now widely accepted that these changes have been caused by human activity.

compact fluorescent lights (CFLs)> lightbulbs that help to reduce energy use. CFLs are the same as the well-known fluorescent tubes, but smaller and shaped differently. They use less energy, don't produce as much heat as standard incandescent lightbulbs, and last up to ten times as long. Because CFLs contain small amounts of mercury, users should check with their local authorities on the best ways to dispose of spent bulbs.

dioxin> the popular name for a group of extremely dangerous organic compounds that can accumulate in the body tissue of humans and animals.

eco-friendly> *eco* comes from *ecology*—the study of living things and how they interact—so *eco-friendly* describes something that does little or no harm to life or to the environment.

ecological footprint> a measure of how much land is needed to provide everything a person, group, city, or country uses. This amount of land also needs to absorb the waste that is created by the people living there. People living in wealthy societies use more resources and, therefore, create more waste than those living in poorer countries, so wealthier societies have larger ecological footprints.

ecotourism> a form of tourism designed to make sure that travelers do not harm the environment in any way. It focuses on naturally beautiful places and aims to provide ways tourists can enjoy the environment and learn how to take care of it.

environmental audit> an assessment of the environmental impact that a person or organization has on the environment.

e-waste> old pieces of electrical equipment, such as cell phones, computers, DVD players, and wires, that people throw away.

food miles> the distance our food travels from where it is grown and harvested to your plate. This term represents the environmental impact of the food we eat. For example, in many cases much of what we eat has traveled great distances—by road or even by air—to reach the grocery store or our table.

fossil fuels> carbon deposits in the earth that were made by billions of animals and plants that lived millions and millions of years ago. Over the centuries these deposits are converted into coal, gas, and oil (which is used to make gasoline). Once humans have used them all up, there will be no more fossil fuels for millions of years.

global warming> the effect that takes place when CO_2 and other greenhouse gases trap heat in Earth's atmosphere. The effect is similar to that which occurs in a greenhouse, which is used in colder weather to grow plants that need warmth and humidity in order to thrive.

greenhouse gas> any atmospheric gas that contributes to the greenhouse effect by absorbing energy from the sun. Naturally occurring greenhouse gases include water vapor, carbon dioxide, methane, nitrous oxide, and ozone. A broad range of human activities, like generating electricity in coal-fired power stations or driving cars, adds to the creation of these substances.

green power> electricity generated from renewable sources—such as water, wind, and solar power—that do not emit greenhouse gases.

greenwashing> the actions of a company, government, or other organization that engages in misleading or untrue practices relating to the environment or to green practices, benefits, and outcomes of a product or service. This concept is derived from the term *whitewashing*.

hybrid engine> an engine that has more than one source of power, usually a gasoline engine and an electric motor that work together more efficiently than one power source. A hybrid vehicle can use as little as 1 gallon of fuel for every 50 miles of driving.

Kyoto Protocol> an international agreement on global warming and emissions targets set at the United Nations Conference on Climate Change in Kyoto, Japan, in 1997. The United States is the only industrialized nation that has not yet signed the protocol.

landfill> a method of solid waste disposal in which garbage or trash is buried in the ground between layers of dirt in low-ground or excavated pits (this is also called a dump). It can take many years for the waste to break down, and the process produces methane, which is a greenhouse gas. Landfills sometimes contain dangerous chemicals that can cause pollution, especially if they get into water sources.

methane> a gas with a greenhouse effect 23 times greater than carbon dioxide. Methane is produced naturally from volcanoes, wetlands, termites, and the ocean. A lot of methane also comes from human activity, such as the decomposition of organic trash buried in landfills, and from gas given off by cattle and sheep.

organic> describing something that is produced naturally, without fertilizers made from fossil fuels, artificial pesticides, or genetically modified crop varieties.

oxygen> a gas that makes up one-fifth of the air we breathe. It is colorless, tasteless, and scentless, and all living things need it to survive. The oxygen we breathe today was first formed millions of years ago by the earliest species of plant life in the oceans.

petrochemical> a chemical made from a component of petroleum or natural gas. Common petrochemicals include benzene, ammonia, acetylene, and polystyrene. Petrochemicals are widely used in agriculture and in the manufacture of plastics, soaps and detergents, solvents, drugs, fertilizers, pesticides, explosives, synthetic fibers and rubbers, paints, epoxies, and flooring and insulating materials.

photosynthesis> the process in which sunlight converts water and CO_2 into food for a plant, and oxygen is then released as a waste product.

plastic code> a number identifying the most common plastic type in a product or package. All plastics marked 1 to 7 are recyclable, but in practice many are not:

1> polyethylene terephthalate (PET)
2> high-density polyethylene (HDPE)
3> unplasticized polyvinyl chloride (UPVC) or plasticized polyvinyl chloride (PPVC)
4> low-density polyethylene (LDPE)
5> polypropylene (PP)
6> polystyrene (PS) or expandable polystyrene (EPS)
7> other, including nylon and acrylic

post-consumer recycled> made from materials previously used as a consumer item that has been recycled by the consumer (by placing it in commercial or residential recycling programs or by reusing it).

renewable energy> energy that is produced from sources, like wind, sun, or water, that are naturally replenished rather than those whose resources are limited, such as fossil fuels.

solar-powered> driven by the transformation of sunlight into electricity.

sustainability> the ability to provide materials that are needed now without using resources that will be required for future needs.

volatile organic chemicals (VOCs or organic gases)> substances emitted as gases from certain solids or liquids. Organic chemicals are normally ingredients in many thousands of products that we use or are surrounded by in our everyday lives—at home (cosmetics, cleaning supplies, disinfectants, furnishings); in buildings (building materials, paints, varnishes); in the office (copiers, printers, correction fluid, permanent markers); and in the garden or toolshed (fuels, paint strippers, pesticides, and hobby products). Concentrations of VOCs are up to ten times higher indoors than outdoors.

waste management> reducing the amount of trash going into landfills through more efficient use of materials, reducing waste, recycling, and reusing discarded materials.

Clean up the world

about Clean Up the World

Clean Up the World, the international outreach campaign of Clean Up Australia, was co-founded by *True Green* creator Kim McKay and Ian Kiernan, AO—legendary yachtsman and 1994 Australian of the Year.

In partnership with the United Nations Environment Programme (UNEP), Clean Up the World annually attracts more than 35 million volunteers who join community-led initiatives to clean up, fix up, and conserve their local environment.

Fifteen years after its launch, the campaign has become a successful action program that spans more than 120 countries, encouraging communities to take control of their own destiny by improving the health of their community and environment.

Global activities include waste collection, education campaigns, environmental concerts, creative competitions, and exhibitions on improving water quality, planting trees, minimizing waste, reducing green house gas emissions, and establishing recycling centers.

Participants range from whole countries (e.g., Australia and Poland), community and environmental groups, schools, government departments, businesses, consumer and industry organizations, to sponsors and dedicated individuals who either work independently in their local communities or with other groups in a coordinated effort at a regional or national level.

Visit the Clean Up the World website to find out how your community, company, or organization can become involved: **www.cleanuptheworld.org**

"For more than 15 years Clean Up the World has empowered individuals to take care of our environment. The work of our volunteers has made and will continue to make significant inroads, but now it's time to move to the next stage and address the significant environmental threats that face us today in the key areas of climate change, waste and water."

Ian Kiernan, AO
Chairman & Founder, Clean Up the World

Photo: Marc Stanley, titomedia

Kim McKay (right), is co-founder of Clean Up Australia and Clean Up the World. An international social and sustainability marketing and communications consultant and principal of Momentum2, Kim counts National Geographic among her clients.

Jenny Bonnin (left) is a director of Clean Up Australia and Clean Up the World and Sydney representative of the Clinton Climate Initiative. Jenny has two children and lives with her partner and extended family.

Both Kim and Jenny live in Sydney, Australia.

Marian Kyte is a freelance designer and creative director of True Green. She has a passion for incorporating sustainability principles into her work and her life. Her clients have included Qantas, Craftsman House Books, Power Publications, Sherman Galleries, *Art & Australia*, *Limelight* magazine, and True Green. Her son Locky is her eternal inspiration.

Helen Littleton is an editor and researcher with a book publishing career spanning more than 20 years. She first collaborated with True Green as an editor on *True Green Home*. Her commitment to the environment has been inspired by the desire for a more sustainable world for her three children, Astrid, Alex, and Max.

acknowledgments

True Green Life is the culmination of our four previous books and has been the opportunity to weave the concept of living a true green life into the fabric of our daily activities in a practical and simple way. This series and book *True Green Life* would not have been possible without the generous creative spirit and talents of designer Marian Kyte, who has been a great friend and inspiration. Color, simple design, and a joyful approach are central to Marian's professional and personal life.

Editing, insight, and words come together in Helen Littleton's work, and we are greatly appreciative of her experience, professional approach, and dedication to this book. As ever, we are grateful to another key member of our True Green team, Kathy Stark, who has interpreted the text for the American audience.

Nina Hoffman, Barbara Brownell Grogan, and Amy Briggs of National Geographic Books have all been great champions. We'd also like to acknowledge the work of business writer Tim Wallace, as some of the points have been sourced from our earlier book *True Green @ Work*.

Special thanks to the Clean Up team—especially Clean Up the World's Tricia Wilden and the entire hardworking staff.

This book is dedicated to our environmental heroes: Tim Flannery, Al Gore, David Suzuki, Laurie David, Ray Anderson, Peter Garrett, Molly Harriss Olson, Philip Toyne, Alan Tate, Mark Lynas, and Ian Kiernan, as they provided the inspiration to keep on pushing the true green message every day.

Treat the Earth well: it was not given to you by your parents,
it was loaned to you by your children.
We do not inherit the Earth from our ancestors,
we borrow it from our children.

—Ancient proverb